"Get My Glory Back in My House"

How to Practice the Presence of
God for the True Worshippers

By

Dr. Jennifer Gaither

"Get My Glory Back in My House"

How to Practice the Presence of God for the True Worshippers

By

Dr. Jennifer Gaither

JenRod Publishing

All Biblical references, quotes, and translations are taken from the King James Version of the Holy Bible.

"Get My Glory Back in My House'
Copyright © 2012 by Dr. Jennifer Gaither

For information or to contact the author, address correspondence to:

JenRod Publishing, Inc.
6107 Hopeton Avenue
Baltimore, Maryland 21215
(410) 358-3360

Library of Congress Control Number 2012916956

ISBN: 0-9664154-2-6

First Edition
54321

Dedication

This book is dedicated to:

The saints who thirst for God but don't know where to begin look for Him.

The saints who are running after God and have not yet found Him.

The saints whom God has found and are looking to go higher.

The saints who are looking for instructions to help others who are seeking more of God.

The leadership of congregations who truly want God's glory present in the worship experience.

The body of Christ who is tired of "playing church" and desires more intimacy with Christ.

The body of Christ who desires to have a mountaintop experience every time they worship privately or with the saints.

Acknowledgements

This project was a major undertaking for me. I thank the Almighty Jehovah for creating me to be a worshipper. I believe that this is the highest calling that a Christian can attain. When you are a worshipper, your heart beats in sync with the Holy Spirit and that is a good thing. I thank Jesus, my Lord and Savior, for allowing me to sit in His presence at His feet to learn of Him. I ran after Him, and He caught me in worship. Words do not express what it means to be connected to the one who died for me. The Holy Spirit came and filled my spirit with the concepts to share in this book. He told me how to break them down so that the reader could truly grasp the knowledge. He spoke and I wrote. Thank you, Holy Spirit, for being my teacher and giving me the book title.

I thank my husband, Roddy, for publishing this book and for understanding the hours that I put into writing it, as I sat at the computer throughout the night. I thank my daughter, Rhoshon, who shares my passion for worship and who gave me the sub-title for the book. I thank my former student, Brian Ray, who helped me with the formatting of the book and has always come to my aide whenever I requested help. Finally, I thank Dr. Charsetta Grant,

---

a sister in Christ, for formatting the design for the book cover in such a timely fashion.

It has been my joy to share with the reader the awesome privilege I have experienced in my quest to draw closer to God. It is difficult to help bring someone out of something that you have never experienced yourself. I have sat in the same seat that many Christians sit in now. I know what it is to be in bondage. I thank Jesus for setting me free. I look for God in every place I go. I am still searching for a higher and deeper revelation of who He is. I pray that my passion never fades away but will act as a catalyst to assist other saints in their journey to reach out to God. Remember, your job is to run and seek. The job of the Holy Spirit is to find you. The place where He finds you is in worship.

Introduction

I thank Jehovah for impressing upon me to write this much needed guide that worship leaders, pastors, and the saints can glean from as they make it their quest to enter into the presence of God. I thank you Jesus for saving me and allowing me to sit in your presence. I thank the sweet Holy Spirit for moving upon me to help me write this book. This book is not deep, but it is practical and doable. There are no new revelations but foundational truths, which allows the believer to come to grips with where they want their relationship with God to progress. I believe the single most important step after a Christian is saved is to receive the baptism of the Holy Spirit, who will then help them to gain access to the manifested presence of God. He alone is your ticket to commune with Jesus. Jesus is the way to the Father, and the Holy Spirit is the way to the presence of Jesus. Each member of the Godhead works in conjunction with the other. Each member is separate but work as a team. Each is different in function but equal in power (1 John 5:7).

I have been running after God now for over twenty years. After Jesus filled me with the Holy Spirit and I discovered that He would come and meet with me in my home, I yearned for more of Him in my personal time of prayer and meditation. Initially, I thought that His presence would only manifest during a worship service with other believers present. However, I came to understand that it is not where we worship, nor our posture, but the purity and condition of the heart that is more important. Jesus is seeking those who are willing to bare their souls and desire an honest relationship with Him. Jesus alluded to this when He spoke with the Samaritan woman at the well. She basically said that her forefathers worshipped at the temple in Jerusalem. Jesus told her that the day would and had arrived that the real worshippers would worship God in spirit and in truth (John 4:21-24).

I was totally shocked when His Spirit fell on me while I was singing to Jesus one morning. It took me some time to recreate that environment where the Holy Spirit would allow me to sit in God's presence. Even then it was a hit or miss, but I never gave up, for "**...In Thy presence there is fullness**

of joy and at Thy right hand there are pleasures forever more (Psalm 16:11). His joy would sweep over me, and His glory would saturate me. My thirst for Him was so strong that I kept coming back for more. For you see, I had tasted and seen that the Lord was good (Psalm 34:8). Once you have tasted of His goodness and bask in His presence, you will yearn for more of Him. Only His presence can quench that hunger and thirst.

Adam enjoyed a place of fellowship and intimacy with His Creator. Moses experienced it and was forever transformed. A believer cannot live in God's glory without being changed. Some only experience His presence once a week, and others rarely experience it even during worship. Still, others have never experienced the manifested presence of God, and this is very sad. I am speaking about more than a warm feeling. I am speaking of God's presence consuming you. God's presence is accessible to all, but only the true worshippers can tap in to that presence. The true worshippers are those saints who are running after God. They want God to find them, and this reunion takes place in His presence during worship. They are in tune with the Holy Spirit. Occasionally, God will move in a sovereign way, and all who are present can experience His presence. His presence is where all of His children should desire to be and live daily. Fellowshipping together as a body to minister to God and then experiencing His manifested presence is the most important act the church can do collectively. The presence of God is more important than the preached word, taking up offerings, or hearing the choir sing. Jesus died so that God could reestablish a relationship with His people and restore the connection that was lost because of man's sin.

As I visit many churches, I have observed that many pastors cannot discern the presence of God and leave this portion of the service to someone else. Others know that there should be more happening in their services but can only hope that they stumble upon it. Still, there are others who try to force the congregation into His presence through guilt, hype, and fakery. Many believers will throw themselves into an emotional frenzy to please the pastor or praise leader but never really tap into God's presence. I have been in services where enthusiasm, shouting, and noise are all demonstrated, but the people themselves are unchanged. It's almost like they are putting on a show to demonstrate their zeal and fervor for God without actually experiencing God. It is my belief that pastors should first be worshippers themselves, so they can discern what it really taking places in their meetings.

Jehovah is a God of protocol, but His process is not difficult. The veil has been torn and His children have access to Him. The only veil that remains is our flesh. We, as Christians, are responsible for taking care of the flesh issue. Praise and worship moves the flesh out of the way so that we can come into God's presence. Paul stated, **"That no flesh should glory in His presence"** (1 Corinthians 1:29). In order for our spirit to connect to the Holy Spirit, pride, issues, and sin must be acknowledged and confessed, for God will not contaminate Himself by manifesting His presence in a sinful atmosphere. We must come to Him in a humble way by consecrating ourselves to Him and confessing any sin. Then we are free to enter into His gates with thanksgiving and into His courts with praise, to be thankful unto Him and bless His name

(Psalm 100:4-5). Many Christians take issue with this. They know that they are living in sin, and so they just fake the whole experience. God is Holy and we must be honest with Him. Some have just not put in the time necessary to get into God's presence, while others do not know what the presence of God even looks like. I have been at fellowships where I was worshipping the Almighty God, and someone came over to me to console me, as if I were grieving over an issue. All that I was doing was reverencing God. Actually, they were a distraction for me. Saints see tears and assume that you are having problems. They do not recognize what a true worshipper even looks like. I will address this in a later chapter.

It is my belief that during the worship experience, we should be taught the rudiments of worship and then to practice at home until we develop a lifestyle of worship. Worship is not something we just do during a service, but rather a state of mind where we desire to live and connect to our God, and that should be daily or as often as possible. In the natural, we feed our bodies with nourishment daily, and there are many who do feast on the Word; in the manifested presence of God, the impossible is doable, and your level of faith is increased. Your spirit man is rubbing shoulders with The Almighty.

The question is: "Do we really want more of God?" I'm not speaking about going to more conferences or revivals. Many feel that the way to God's presence is by increasing their activities. Of course, God's presence can be found there. But may I suggest that a one-on-one experience will take you much further. You can find God at a conference, but some believe that you have to go to that conference again to acquire the same experience. If you learn to tap into God's presence with a made-up mind and a pure heart anytime, then you can begin to understand what it takes to gain access to His presence. Are you satisfied with just a little dose? If the hunger is not there, then you will simply go through the motions and do what you are required to do without ever experiencing the real presence of God. His presence will make you bow, kneel, or lay prostrate before Him. Read 2 Chronicles 5:1-14 to get a picture of what God's glory looks like. The choir was singing and the musicians were playing, and God's glory came in like a thick cloud that filled the temple and the priests could not stand up to minister. If the saints only knew what they were missing, they would run to get into His presence. The Holy Spirit is not pushy, He is a gentleman. He will not make you do anything against your will. God wants us to pant after Him (Psalm 42:1). He created us for His good pleasure (Rev 4:11). My prayer is that you pray to the Father to increase your hunger and longing for Him.

This book is designed to show leaders what their attitude should be in terms of leading the saints into the presence of God, how to lead them, the difference between praise and worship, what praise and worship should look like, and how to press in to enter into the very presence of God. God has led me through many experiences with Him, so you could say that I have been instructed by the Holy Spirit. You can never unlearn what God has taught you. You can disagree with man, but not God. So I learned my lessons well. I also discovered other worshippers who felt the same way that I did. We had the same views about God and needed time to express those feeling to God. The worship service was not enough. An active prayer life was not enough. We needed time to connect to God in a real way and not out of a sense of duty or just putting in the time. We should desire to see more of our God and to allow His glory to melt us down to a point where we can continuously say yes to Him. So I write this book from the perspective of a worshipper and the commonalities that exist in worship services, which clearly defines those services that truly usher in the presence of God.

This book is not a formula, because we are individuals and God deals with us as individuals. You see, a formula most work the same way every time to achieve the desired result. You may require different music or songs. The language that you speak to God might include different vocabulary. God is not a cookie-cutter God. He is creative. He doesn't like to do the same thing the same way all the time. If you look for Him to come in the same way, you'll miss Him. This book is a guide to help keep you on track. Some of you will not need instruction in every chapter. I do believe that everyone who reads this book can learn something, no matter what level of ministry you are in. It is written under the unction and guidance of the Holy

Spirit to whom I am eternally grateful. "**It is not by might, nor by power, but by my Spirit sayeth the Lord of Host**" (Zechariah 4: 6).

Table of Contents

Chapter 1
My Testimony

God gifted me with a singing voice that I
discovered early on in life. I distinctly remember
singing for my family at the age of six. I sang in
church, in the school's choirs, and I also sang solos
in school programs. I always received positive
feedback on my voice, so I believed I could sing
well. I sang in choirs at all grade levels, including
college. I also formed a quartet in high school called
"The Eldorados." I was the lead soprano as we sang
for community gatherings and social functions. I
sang duets with a good friend at church functions.
In high school, I entered every talent show that I
saw advertised. There was a compelling force that

---

drove me to sing even though I was quite nervous singing in front of people because I feared hitting a wrong note. During my sophomore year at Coppin State Teacher's College, I was given the opportunity to sing with The Count Basis Orchestra, which was a most memorable event for me.

Although I sang in all music genres, which included barbershop quartet, opera, secular, Broadway, and religious, my genre of choice was jazz. Ten years after I graduated from college, I began singing for the Dennis Fisher Band when I was thirty-two years old. I enjoyed it, and it was fulfilling for me. I had a duel career of teaching language arts and performing. I worked for this band for fifteen years, hoping to get a break and enter the world of entertainment on a higher level. But this never happened, because God had other plans for me.

Through the years prior to joining the band, I had been searching for God outside of the Baptist denomination. I became quite interested in the Holy Spirit and began a quest of finding out who He was. In the tenth year of working with this band, one of the band members gave me several tapes on the baptism of the Holy Ghost, speaking in tongues, and faith. As I studied the tapes over a period of a month and through much prayer, I decided that I wanted to be filled with the Holy Ghost with the evidence of speaking in tongues. I had learned that this infilling would give me power to overcome sin, and I would become a bold witness for Christ, and the Spirit would lead and guide me into all truths. Isn't it wonderful to know that God does not change? For the Word of God says that you should **"Ask and it shall be given you, seek, and ye shall find; knock, and it shall be opened unto you"** (Matthew 7:7).

I felt like I could not lose with the power of God residing inside of me. Although I had asked Jesus to come into my heart when I was eleven, now that I was forty-two, I knew I did not have this power to overcome sin and to witness for Christ within me. Over the course of three weeks after studying the word and much prayer, I sought the Lord for the baptism of the Holy Ghost from 7:00p.m. to 7:30 p.m. I was compelled to diligently seek God on a regular basis. I told God that He might as well give

---

it to me, because I was going to bug Him until He did.

This baptism did not occur while I was on my knees yielding to the Spirit, but one evening after purchasing a dress on sale. I was light hearted and began to sing "la la la" while entering my car, and the "la la la" turned into my prayer language, which I continued to speak all the way home. I had full control of the car but not my tongue. The syllables that came were not any that I had spoken before. My heart was racing as I was overcome with joy. I knew that I had hit the jackpot. This was a turning point in my life, because God responded to a request, and I was reassured for the first time that God hears and answers prayer. I knew from that point on that I was on to something big. Over the next few months, God used this powerful moment to deliver me from fear of public worship. The Baptist church where I was raised was very reserved and totally believed that we should, "**Be still and know that I am God**" (Psalm 46:10). I had never felt the manifested presence of God before, for I was taught that God should be respected with order and silence. Little did I know that one day I would exhort others to worship God from the fruit of their lips.

God is the master planner and does everything in a purposeful manner. During this three-week period of seeking God for the infilling of the Holy Ghost, I had made a request of God, and He answered my prayer. During the next big event in my spiritual growth, God required something of me. I love God's uniqueness and His ability to define and redefine one moment to suit our express needs for a greater purpose. For the first time, the Holy Spirit gave me an unction to attend a neighborhood church, which I had passed hundreds of times. As I entered the sanctuary, I began to weep, but I didn't know why. I didn't know the song, and I might not have even understood what they were saying. All I knew was that I felt good, and I wanted to return. I have come to understand that it was God's anointing for a future setup.

When I returned to the same church the next Sunday, the congregation was engaged in praise and worship. Many people stood, while others held their arms up with their palms uplifted to the heavens.

This was when the Holy Spirit made His move. He said to me, "You can clap your hands."

I answered, "But they are looking at me."

He answered, "But didn't I fill you with my Spirit like you asked?"

I answered, "Yes, Lord," and I clapped my hands.

The next Sunday the same exchange transpired. This time the Holy Spirit asked me to lift my hands. I responded the same way, and again He told me that He had done what I'd asked Him to do. This time I lifted my hands. On the third Sunday, the Holy Spirit requested that I stand and lift my hands. I responded again that people were looking at me, and He responded in the same fashion. I said, "Yes, Lord," and stood up with my hands lifted. You would have thought that I would have caught on by now, but I didn't. The Holy Spirit was ever so patient with me. My deliverance was drawing nigh, but not yet complete. Finally, on the forth Sunday, The Holy Spirit told me that I could stand up, clap my hands, and sway to the beat of the music. I answered in the same way, and He responded with the same message.

He said, "Didn't I do what you asked me to do?"

I said, "Yes Lord." I stood up and swayed, as I clapped my hands and was totally set free. From that point on, I have never failed to give God visible and audible praise for what He had done and to worship Him for being God. I always follow the lead of the praise and worship leader, and then allow the Holy Spirit to take over. This was all done by the hand of God. When God reveals something, you can never unlearn it. He truly is the master teacher. I knew how it felt to be bound, and I had been set free. Freedom was better. **"And ye shall know the truth, and the truth shall make you free"** (John 8:32).

The Holy Spirit had me practice the presence of God. This was a course in Praise 101. 101 courses always give you the basics so you can familiarize yourself with the concept. What the Holy Spirit taught me was basic and foundational. I learned more as the course progressed. I was engaged in biblical actions based upon the reality of who God is and what He had done for me. These two actions set me free. I'm still asking the Holy Spirit to take me higher. Only those who hunger and thirst after righteousness shall be filled (Matthew 5:6).

After my infilling, I was able to be a greater witness for Christ. I was able to bring teachers, students, and parents to Christ. Jesus was glorified in my school's programs. Jesus was truly Lord in all the schools that I worked in, and many students that I taught would come to me for prayer. Everyone knew that I was sold out to Christ.

In 2003, I was diagnosed with stage four colon cancer. I went through surgery and eight rounds of chemotherapy. The effects of the chemo were very bad, and I retired early from teaching. I could not tolerate the cold in the winter or the air conditioning in the summer. For about four years I stayed home and worshipped God every day. This day-to-day experience made me more sensitive to the Holy Spirit. I thrived as a worshipper because I allowed the Holy Spirit to completely take control of my spirit. The results were astounding. Entering into

God's presence took little effort. I began dancing during worship at different churches under the unction of the Holy Spirit. God used me in different ways such as praying, singing, exhorting, and even a prophetic utterance. I was an empty vessel ready to be filled and used by the Holy Spirit over and over at His command. The Holy Spirit continues to refill your vessel as you empty out in service to God. I never know how the Holy Spirit will use me from day-to-day. My journey thus far has been an awesome one.

This book is a result of time spent with the Holy Spirit. After years of worshipping God, the mandate came from Him to teach other Christians, who were hungry for more, to worship Him. This is a book written out of obedience to my Savior.

There are several levels of praise, and the congregation needs to be reminded at each service what praise and worship means through demonstration and participation. The people must be taught why they are being asked to do certain things during the worship service and a connection made to the one they are worshipping. Many congregations are deep in tradition and must be delivered. They need to be shown that the raising of the hands, clapping, shouting, dancing, singing, exhorting, and bowing are all actions exhibited in the Old Testament during worship. God has not changed. These actions are necessary to help propel us into the presence of God. It's the first step to help us put our flesh under subjection so that our spirit can commune with God.

God is still God and desires that His creation give Him praise and His disciples worship Him. The Word of God declares that we overcome the accuser by the blood of the lamb and the word of our testimony (Rev. 12: 11). I pray that my testimony will inspire you to desire the deeper things of God so that He might empower you with more revelation of Him. As you walk in the truth of the light that is given to you, God will reveal more. If you run from the light, you will remain in darkness. Peter declared, "…**God is no respecter of persons** (Acts 10: 34). What He does for others, He'll do for you. God is looking and waiting for the true worshippers to pant after Him (Psalm 42:1).

Chapter 2
Why Should We Praise and Worship God?

In the Bible, God says that He is the first and the last. He is the beginning and the end. This means that there was none before Him, nor will there be any to come after Him. This is awesome. Revelation 4:11 declares, **"Thou art worthy, O Lord, to receive glory and honor and power: for Thou hast created all things, and for thy pleasure they were created."** We were created to please God. He, therefore, has the right to demand praise from His creation. God does not need us to exist, but we need Him to exist. The invisible God created all that is seen and unseen; therefore, there is none greater. Therefore, God expects His creation to pay homage to their Creator. Colossians1:16 states, **"For by him were all things created, that are in the heavens and in the earth, visible and invisible, whether they be thrones or dominions, or principalities or powers: all things were created by Him and for Him."**

There are many other scriptures where God is adamant about His creation showing reverence to Him. Psalm 150:6 declares, **"Let everything that hath breath praise the Lord. Praise ye the Lord."** God desires to be acknowledged by His creation even though they do not serve Him. To those who serve Him, Paul declares in Hebrew13:15, **"By Him therefore let us offer up the sacrifice of praise to God continually, that is, the fruit of our lips giving thanks to His name."** Yes, we are to sing praises to His name, but we also should be able to offer up praises from our hearts through our lips. We should be able to talk to God and tell Him how great He really is. He says you must praise me. God requires it. Shouldn't that be enough?

God also wants His children to be thankful for His provisions and His protection. Remember the

Israelites wandering in the wilderness for forty years? They murmured and complained after God had delivered them from bondage. They were delivered but did not have the dainties that they were accustomed to having, and so they forgot about their deliverance and focused on the things they did not have. This is just what Christians do at times. God was testing Israel to give an example for us today about the proper gratitude we should have for our Deliverer (Exodus 16: 1-3). Did God deliver you from anything? Remember, I just shared with you how God delivered me from fear of worshipping Him in public. My Baptist upbringing taught me to be silent during the service. The Holy Spirit had to deliver me. It's easy to forget where you have been, because you are no longer in the same condition. Praising God reminds us of the things He delivered us from. Psalm 148 actually demands all of creation from the heavens to the mountains, from hail to the wind to praise Him. Verse 14 says, **"For His name alone is excellent and his glory is above the earth and the heavens."** God created us to praise Him and be grateful for His love and mercy. Praise is an act of obedience.

Praise also can produce power. In 2 Chronicles, Chapter 20, we see God's plan for Jehoshaphat to win the battle against the Moabites and the Ammonites. The plan called for the singers to go before the army with praises unto God.

> **And when he had consulted with the people, he appointed singers unto the Lord, and that should praise the beauty of holiness, as they went out before the army, and to say, 'Praise the Lord: for His mercy endureth forever'. And when they began to sing and to praise, the Lord set ambushments against the children of Ammon, Moab, and Mount Seir, which were come against Judah; and they were smitten**(2 Chronicles 21-22).

God performed a miracle through Jehoshaphat's obedience. The enemy was expecting a fight, not singers singing praises to God. God still uses this strategy today to confuse the enemy when we are attacked. Praise produces power by confusing the enemy. When we praise God while we are in the battle or struggle, Satan is confused by this action and withdraws from the attack. How great is our God? He uses the simple things to give us victory. If you are going through a trial, this is a good time to praise God.

In Psalm 22: 3, David declares, **"But thou art holy, O thou that inhabitest the praises of Israel."** God dwells in our praise. Our praise summons God and gets His attention. Praise is where God lives. **"For the eyes of the Lord run to and fro throughout the earth, to shew himself strong in the behalf of them whose heart is perfect toward Him"** (2 Chronicles 16). So, we as believers should desire to praise God with clean hearts because God is searching for those who desire Him. He has something special for those whom He finds that are thirsty for Him.

Worship is praise but on a higher level. In *Strong's Concordance*, worship (*shachah* in Hebrew) and (*proskuneo* in Greek) means to bow, crunch, and humbly beseech, to make obeisance to a god, reverence, to stoop, lie prostrate or lie flat. This act or positioning of the body reflects a sign of humility where one becomes smaller to denote the greatness or largeness of the deity being worshipped. This outward action should be an indicator of what is happening in the heart. In our society rarely does a man bow before another man. However, this practice still exists in countries where there are kingdoms and kings or royalty. Because Jesus is the King of Kings, such reverence would be expected. The deity or ruler would of course be powerful, wealthy, and have a people dependent upon His protection and His provisions for making a living. In the natural, a king becomes powerful because he has overpowered all of his enemies and has the means to put to death anyone who does not obey him or his statutes. This type of worship was expected with dire consequences for not participating. Most people would actually fear the king for having such power over them, so they would worship him. Fear is one of the greatest motivators for worshipping an earthly king.

God was once feared by His creation. He was a God of wrath, as well as a God of blessings. Jesus was God's way of introducing grace. This undeserved favor from God is the message of the

---

gospel. Man found it difficult to obey God. God devised a way for man to actually walk in truth and holiness by supernaturally living inside of the believer through the born again experience and infilling of the Holy Ghost, who gives direction and conviction. With this supernatural power living inside of us, sin is revealed and dealt with. In God's presence, it's easy to say yes. God does not want His children to fear Him but to be motivated by His love for us and our love toward Him. God demonstrated His love toward us through Jesus (Romans 5:8) to leave no doubt in our minds about this new covenant. So we should be running to get into the presence of God and not shrugging away. Communing with God daily will reveal error, sin, motives, and then power to overcome.

As we get into God's presence, His glory saturates our total being, and we are compelled to desire to live a life that is pleasing to Him. Our spirit man is repelled by our sin and the Holy Spirit empowers us to live holy. We need God's presence to be the overcomers that we say we are. This can not be done once a week during a two-hour service. More time is spent on teaching why we should give and tithe and a short time exhorting the people to worship. If more time were given on how to enter into God's presence through praise and worship and actually allow the Holy Spirit to do His work, there would be a greater desire to obey the Word of God, and sin would become less pervasive. Our pastors often become enablers to the congregation, and the people rely more upon the leadership instead of the Holy Spirit. We just need to let God be God. Our job is to create the climate conducive to the workings of the Holy Spirit.

As a result of David's writing of the Psalms, we as believers see God through the eyes of Christ. We see a God of love, mercy, and grace. David showed us another dimension of God—not just one to be feared but revered, loved, and cherished. Real worship is birthed out of relationship, not fear. Real worship is adoration, not ritual. David showed us the heart of God on a personal level. He saw God as his help, protection, his joy, and his love. Then God came in the likeness of flesh as Christ and dwelled among the people and proved Himself to be a teacher, a friend, and a Savior. The more you can acknowledge your need for God, your love for God, and your excitement about God, the deeper the worship experience becomes.

God is a God of process, and He did not reveal Himself totally to His creation at one time but in stages. Adam communed with God from spirit to Spirit. He did not have to practice the presence of God, for it was as natural as eating and sleeping. Then sin separated man from God, and man lost the ability to fellowship the way he had once enjoyed. Through the ages, God devised a way to reconnect to man so that the day-to-day fellowship could be restored. The Ark of the Covenant, Tabernacle, and Temple worship were all shadows to lead us back to fellowship with our Creator. God only dwelled in these special places. Now, His children have become the temple of God, for He comes to dwell in the hearts of men when we receive Jesus as Lord. Jesus is the only way back to God. Our freedom was paid with an awesome price, which was the blood of Jesus.

Many resist this intimacy that God desires. They prefer God to be afar. We see the same parallel during Moses' leadership with Israel in Exodus

20:19, **"And they said unto Moses, Speak thou with us and we will hear: but let not God speak with us, lest we die."** God gave the Ten Commandments with thunder and lightning and the people were afraid. They preferred that their leader communicate with God and then relay the message.

So it is today. Many are afraid of communing with God on a personal level. They would rather let the preacher commune with God on their behalf. What about you? Do you really hunger for a fresh encounter with the living God? We allow sin to continue to separate us from the presence of God instead of confessing the sin and crying out to God to deliver us from ungodly behavior. Some are afraid of being real with God and continue to hide themselves from God. This is why Jesus died for our sins. We have already been set free by His blood, but some are afraid to walk in this liberty. Jesus' work has been completed. It is now up to each believer to walk in the light that has been given to us. The way back to the light and intimacy is through worship. Worship bares the soul and takes restraints off the mind and the flesh. Worship is getting naked before God. It allows our soul and spirit to be flooded with the power of the Holy Spirit. Worship can only be done through our spirits. We need the Holy Spirit to open up our spirit in order to connect to God. The flesh must decrease so the mind can be totally focused on God, and then the Holy Spirit will seize that moment to pull our spirit into the very presence of God...

Chapter 3
What Does Praise Look Like?

God is a God of protocol. We do not approach Him
in just any way. Through the death of His son Jesus
Christ, we no longer have to follow a ritual where
other people must be involved in order for us to
connect with God, but we do need to clear the
atmosphere. In tabernacle worship from the Old
Testament, incense was burned daily to create a
sweet smelling fragrance for God. God lives in the
third heavens. If we want God to meet up with us,
the atmosphere must be clean and charged with
praise. Our praise becomes a sweet aroma. Singing
a song alone does not charge the atmosphere. Since
God inhabits the praises of His people (Psalm 22:3),
much praise must be lifted from the fruit of our lips

for God to meet with us (Hebrews 13:15). You could say that praise is where God will come to live. We know God receives praise in heaven continuously. God is omnipresent, and he can be everywhere at the same time. He is attracted to our praise and will come to dwell in it. Wherever God resides must be clean and holy. He will not contaminate Himself by coming to a sinful atmosphere. This atmosphere must be charged with praise. Our praise creates space for Him to come and sit in our presence.

It is good when we come together to worship as a community, but I would say that it would be better for each of God's children to practice the presence so that when we gather, the glory of God will rain down more powerfully. We can worship God whenever and wherever we so desire. It's good to hear the choir sing, musicians play, and the praise leader exhort, but the Word of God says that we are all priests in the Kingdom. When God sees His child reaching out to Him and longing for Him, He desires to respond. What earthly father would deny a child wanting to be picked up and loved? How much more would our Heavenly Father desire to reach out to His children (Luke 11:10-13)? This means that each of us who has received Jesus as our Lord and Savior can come boldly to the throng of grace (Hebrews 4:16). If we want God to manifest or show His presence, we must first clear the atmosphere through praise.

There are some things we do to open our spirits up, so that we can enter into the presence of God to have an enjoyable worship experience. God is a Spirit, and therefore our flesh must be put aside so that our spirits can be free to commune with God (see Figure 1.). Man is more than just flesh. The real you is spirit, which is clothed in flesh, and you have a soul. I Thessalonians 5:23 tells us that man has a spirit, a soul, and a body. Praise will ignite the flesh and soul by removing any hindrances or barriers, such as depression, fatigue, pain, grief, and worry. Isaiah 61:3 tells us to put on the garment of praise for the spirit of heaviness. As long as the mind is dwelling on other issues, the spirit cannot be free. If your mind is focused on Jesus, then these hindrances will be removed. This is why God orchestrated the praise paradigm. God is exalted in praise, and our flesh is put under subjection. Praise is for God, but we benefit also. Praise lifts the mind to a higher dimension. Your thoughts are now on Him, so the protocol goes like this: **"Enter into His Gates with thanksgiving and into His courts with praise. Be thankful unto Him and bless His name, for the Lord is good and His mercy endureth forever"** (Psalm 100:4). There should be an air of excitement and celebration as we come to God with praise and thanksgiving. This means more than just singing a song. There should be an expectation that God wants to see us as much as we want to see Him. True praise is running to God or seeking after God.

Flesh	Soul	Spirit
Connect to the earth through senses	Mind, emotions, personality, thoughts	Connects to the spirit realm through the Holy Spirit
Sight, smell, taste, touch, hearing	Must be transformed by the Word to renew mind to be led by the spirit	Heart is the center and dwelling place of the Holy Spirit

Figure 1.

Now this protocol begins our entrance into His courts. We are on a journey to reach out to God in the holy place to get His glory in the house, but our flesh is in the way. **"God is a Spirit and they that worship Him must worship Him in Spirit and in truth"** (John 4:24). We know God's power can fix us and every situation. We really don't feel like reaching out, because there are so many issues clouding our minds, and our bodies are tired. The voluntary act of praise helps to put the flesh under subjection so that we can connect with God and allow His glory to fill the temple.

Hebrews 13:15 exhorts us to offer up the sacrifice of praise from the fruit of our lips. We no longer have animal sacrifices. God has made it easy for us during this church age. All we need to do is to think on Him and speak praises unto God from our lips. No one else can praise God for us. True praise is a spontaneous burst of utterances that come from deep within our hearts and are released from our lips. This is one of the first acts of worship we can do. We want God's glory or presence in the house. Anything can transpire when God's glory is in the house, such as healing, deliverance, revelation, and salvation. The more we can get on one accord, the greater the glory.

Praising God should not be a difficult thing to do. Has God done anything for you? Did you get that job you applied for? Did God send the man or woman of your dreams? Did you finally conceive the child you were praying for? Are you healthy? Is your eyesight in tact? Were you able to get out of bed on your own? Do you have a sound mind? There are thousands of others who desire to have what God has blessed you with. Find some reasons for which you can thank and praise God. Do you get the picture? When we praise God for the mighty things He has done in our lives, our flesh is subdued and our minds are fixed on Him.

The one thing I have learned from my walk with God is that all of His requirements are really for our benefit. I give or tithe to God, and He supplies all of my needs as well as the needs of others. As we give thanks, praise, and worship to our God, He allows us to sit in His presence, and you cannot get better than that. He requires something from us, and we get blessed when we obey. Sometimes we just need to obey without question and see what the benefits are. Too often we ponder, research, and debate before we get the picture, thereby missing out on the promises or benefits. Many resist because they do not understand and others have not been taught.

In any given service, we see many different theatrics going on during praise and worship of God. The Book of Psalms contains a collection of nuances that the Israelites engaged in as they worshipped. We see the bowing, singing, clapping, shouting, and the lifting of hands to demonstrate the greatness of God. Let's read from the Bible those actions that symbolize praise.

"O clap your hands, all ye people; shout unto God with the voice of triumph" (Psalm 47:1).

"But let all those that put their trust in Thee rejoice: let them ever shout for joy, because thou defendest them: let them also that love thy name be joyful in thee" (Psalm 5:11), and also see Psalm 32:11.

"Sing unto the Lord, O ye saints of His, and give thanks at the remembrance of His holiness" (Psalm 30:4), and also see Psalm 96:1, Psalm 66:2, and Psalm 9:2.

"Let them praise His name in the dance: let them sing praises unto Him with the timbrel and harp" (Psalm 149:3), and also see Psalm 150:4.

"Lift up your hands in the sanctuary, and bless the Lord" (Psalm 134:2).

"And to stand every morning to thank and praise the Lord, and likewise at even" (1 Chronicles 23:30).

"O Come, let us worship and bow down: let us kneel before the Lord our maker" (Psalm 95:6).

Most saints are comfortable with singing and shy away from the other demonstrations of praise such as dancing and hand clapping. When the leadership teaches and demonstrates, the people will follow. Pastors must lead by example. Saints are comfortable demonstrating these behaviors at other functions but not during a worship service. Remember, we are also flesh, and the flesh responds to acts of praise to God very heartily.

Even the world has caught on to this concept. The raising of hands at games, parties, and concerts is very prominent. This gesture signifies that you're "bad" or you're "great." Have you ever heard the noise fans make at a ball game? Do you feel the excitement? Do you see the lifted hands when the favorite team scores? What they are doing is praising their team. This is the atmosphere you want when coming to see the King. You have come to celebrate your Lord and Savior, Jesus Christ.

Praising God is not a spectator sport. It requires participation. No one can praise God for you. The praise you gave yesterday was for yesterday. You need a fresh praise for today. Just like anything else, the more you participate and practice, the easier it becomes. It might appear strange in the beginning when you are not accustomed to high praise, but continue to think about the grace and mercy God gives you everyday. That's enough to shout and rejoice right there.

During an upbeat selection, there would be clapping of hands and swaying from side to side. This happy music generates excitement about God and even the body is in agreement. Now, the believer is elevated to a place in their mind where they are not in worry, pain, or anxiety mode. Our minds are now fixed on the One we adore. The fleshy issues are now being laid to rest. The soul has one thought on its mind— Jesus.

When I am in a service and the songs do not lift up the name of Jesus, I create my own altar and speak words of praise from my own heart. I deviate from the program to attain what I'm seeking. Sometimes, the praise team will sing and repeat a phrase that does not create the picture in my heart that I need. I superimpose my own words that will glorify Christ. Sometimes the praise leader will canter out a word to the congregation with which I disagree. I cannot say I'm "running running, running" over and over in a song directed by the praise leader, but I can say

"I love you, I love you, I love you" over and over or halleluiah. Whatever you say, make sure your mind and heart are staying on Him. Praising while writing a check, checking out someone's praise, or looking at someone's apparel are distractions and will hinder you from entering in.

The songs used for praise are very important. "We are Soldiers in the Army," "Victory is Mine," and "I Need You to Survive" are not praise songs and should be used in other parts of the service. "What a Mighty God We Serve," "God is Great," by Ricky Dillard, "This is the Day That the Lord Hath Made," " Praise Him, Praise Him," "All Hail the Power of Jesus' Name," and "I've Come to Praise His Name." This is just a short list of praise songs. There are hundreds of possibilities. The message should be clear, for the selections used must exalt the Mighty One and Him alone. Some fellowships prefer hymns from a book, but this traditional form keeps the congregation glued to a book, and the believer might find it difficult to let spontaneous praise come forth. My suggestion is to allow the worship leader to canter out the phrases as the congregation repeats. Many contemporary fellowships have a screen up front that displays the words. The leader would select a simple praise song that is easy to grasp as a starting point. Songs from the hymnbook can be sung after the praise and worship experience during other times in the service.

One point to be made here is that the praise leaders should themselves be worshippers. It is hard to lead someone to a place you have never been. Ministers of music, worship leaders, and pastors, along with the other ministers should all be worshippers. Maybe this is where a congregation needs to start. The leadership must be willing to move to a higher place. A worshiper is someone who spends quality time in the presence of God and has a lifestyle of worship. They become vessels used by God to carry the anointing and to lead the people into God's presence.

The praise leader has an awesome responsibility to assist the congregation in leading them to the throng. This should not be done through badgering the congregation and making them feel guilty. Sometimes, congregants will appease the worship leader by appearing to give the leader what he wants. Their mouths are open, but they are doing others things, such as adjusting their hair, going through their handbags, and preparing their offering. This type of fakery will not work. If their praise is not from the heart, it will not do what it is suppose to do anyway. Yelling and coercion will not work, and it only brings in a spirit of anger and irritation. Now the service is being counter productive. Your goal is to get as many people as possible on one accord. You are looking for a Pentecostal or mountaintop experience, where God comes down and tabernacles with His people. Instead, many in the congregation are mad and they shut down, go to the restroom, or just chill out. It's not how loudly the congregation is singing, but rather if they are praising from their hearts. I will reiterate here that the purpose of gathering to worship is to see God in all of His splendor and allow Him to touch the people with His glory so that they may be transformed in some way.

The leader should not get louder and force the congregation to be more involved. The leader should lower the music and give a short explanation of what we are trying to accomplish here. I would say to the people that if you are tired and weary, just sit while the rest of the congregation continues. The bottom line is that if the congregation continues to resist the leadings of the worship leader, the pastor should do a series of teachings to open up the hearts of the people for change. Within those teachings, the pastor should remind the congregation of why they are in fellowship and what he hopes to achieve collectively while each believer is there. It's all about needing their help to usher in the presence of God, so that He will meet their needs. This is paramount! The worship leaders are there to help the saints get a glimpse of God. Ask them! Do you want to see God's glory or participate in a program? Jesus should be the star attraction. If He is not in the house, why are you gathered together anyway?

Since each congregation is led by a pastor or under-shepherd, the people need a model to demonstrate what praise and worship should look like. Pastors should participate in the worship experience. Many congregants have never seen their pastor do what they are required to do. It gives out the wrong message when pastors enter the pulpit after the praise and worship service has finished. The pastor ought to be personally involved at some point in the worship service. The people need to see their leader submitting himself to God in this act of free will and humility. There is no double standard here, but authentic surrendering to the Most High God.

The leader should also allow the people to give spontaneous praises from the fruit of their lips and out of the abundance of their hearts without being led. As the music is flowing, let the people praise. The level of the music should not be so loud that the members of the congregation cannot hear themselves praising God. I believe some musicians are instructed to play loudly to compensate for lack of enthusiasm in the singing. This pretense gives the allusion that the people are really putting out. Sometimes the congregation needs to sing a cappella. This will give them the freedom to express what is in their hearts and takes the responsibility off the praise leader. It allows the leader to teach the congregation that they can do this independently of the leader, and that no one needs to pump them up. The people will begin to develop a sense of genuineness in their praise and will not need someone to pump them up. This promotes one-on-one praise.

I would interject here that clapping for the sake of making noise does not take the place of praise from the lips. Clapping has its place to help generate excitement and free the mind to focus on Jesus. However, the leader should lead the people to a point that when the request is given to praise God, the congregation begins to speak out clamorously in response to the request. **"Let us offer the sacrifice of praise to God continually that is the fruit of our lips giving thanks to His name,"** (Hebrews 13:15). I've visited too many fellowships where the clapping takes the place of the outward expressions of vocal praise. Remember, **"Let everything that hath breath praise the Lord,"** (Psalm 150:6). This is what God desires. Any other movements are a means to get to an end.

Praise has several levels. Everyone is not ready to dive into the praise experience. Some come from a traditional background, which excludes vigorous praise. In some congregations, just the act of singing a song is enough praise. Therefore, clapping

---

of hands and foot stomping is seen as being overzealous. That's why teaching is necessary to get an understanding of why we are doing these things. The instruction or teaching should be done gradually with demonstrations so that the congregation can participate with agreement and confidence.

Tradition has taught many that we should be silent when entering into the worship experience, but that does not agree with the Word of God. God says that when you come to worship Me, you should come with praise and thanksgiving. There should be excitement generated by this action as you enter God's presence either alone or in a congregation. We must create an atmosphere for the Holy Spirit to do His work. Our praise and worship creates a seat or platform on our hearts for the Holy Spirit to work to do the will of the Father.

Satan has used tradition to keep God's people from discovering who He really is and what His presence does. It is so sad when you talk to Christians who only know God through the pastor and have never discovered the heart of the true and living God.

Jesus died so that we could reach out to God and He respond. There are those who have never been touched by God and don't know how soothing and peaceful it is to bask in His glory as His anointing sweeps over you.

Many have been robbed of His glory, because they don't have a mind to seek for it themselves. They are content to allow tradition to hold them back for fear of looking undignified. They look at someone being caught up in the Spirit and have decided that they don't want to look like that. I have been asked the question, "Do you know what you look like when you sing?" I have been told that I look like I am in pain. Many black Christians feel that they have been delivered from slavery and that to demonstrate outward expressions of love and adoration to God takes them back to the slave or the jungle mentality. They have allowed their intellect and education to despise outward displays of emotion and jubilation. Because there is no instruction during the service, they never come to know or understand what real worship is.

Most Christians can praise God through song. Many will even lift their hands if asked to do so. The next step could be through the waving or clapping of hands to jubilant music. This should progress to actually speaking to God with spontaneous bursts of shouts and thanksgiving. You must have a language that expresses how you feel about Him and not just what someone else declares. What do you declare?

Christians also express their joy in different ways. Some wave banners and play instruments, while others feel the need to run because God has given them the victory. A final step could be to praise Him through dance. Some dance enthusiastically. Dancing should not be forced or always expected. Some leaders almost insist that the entire congregation dance. This type of dancing can be inspired by the Holy Spirit or as an outward expression of joy or victory, but because you have praised God through the dance does not mean you have entered into His presence. Remember, you are on a journey to find God. You have not yet arrived. When you truly enter into the presence of the living God through worship, you are in awe of Him. Dancing is not the final climax. Worship is the final climax. The act of worship is yielding, consuming, soothing, and adoring. There are those who roll on the floor or shout uncontrollably, but this does not mean they have entered into God's presence. This lack of control might indicate their response to the Holy Spirit moving on them or a show-off mentality. Some congregants become observers and forget that they too should be praising God. If you do not participate, you cannot enter into His presence. Praise should not distract others from the One you are worshipping. Jesus is the main attraction. **"No flesh should glory in His presence"** (I Corinthians 1:29). Exuberant praise should draw others into the praise circle and not to compete with each other.

Demonstrate these examples of praise individually so that the people will not become overwhelmed. The leadership should join in and not just place this assignment on the praise team. Praising God should be a time of excitement and jubilation, with thanksgiving done with full participation by all in attendance. Don't expect everyone to be able to do everything initially, but they should be led by example. Then they can return home and practice alone or with another saint. This can be quite an exciting experience.

I know the Holy Spirit is ministering to someone right now. You know there is more. You know you are missing out on something, but you are content in doing things the same old way. I know because I was stuck and didn't even know it. I didn't know how to praise God. I didn't know how to worship Him. I only knew how to sing a song. Singing a song is not enough. My love for God released me from the snare of tradition. God used my former band member to share with me information through an audio tape on faith and the infilling of the Holy Ghost. Once I cried out to God for truth, He removed the scales from my eyes so that I could see. If you are hungry, your God will not deny you. **"Ask, and ye shall receive; seek, and ye shall fine; knock and it shall be opened unto you"** (Matthew 7:7). He cannot deny you, for God does not lie. Take a page from the Book of David and pant after God (Psalm 42:1) so you can be loosened from the chains of the past that hold your mind in captivity.

Remember, we need to practice the presence of God so that we can give Him the opportunity to meet our needs and His desires for us. Living in His presence is where peace and joy abides. Everything we need is in the presence of God.

Chapter 4
The Language of Praise

Most pastors and ministers of music do not have a problem with the language of praise. However, there are some who might say, "I don't know what to say to God." That's because you are not accustomed to praising God. You pray to God, but you don't praise Him from the depths of your heart. The Word tells us to hide the Word in our hearts (Psalm 119:11). Many Christians read the Bible, but they don't retain much of it. May I suggest that you read several chapters of the Book of Psalms in the morning and at night out loud? Write your favorite Scripture on the medicine cabinet and recite it as you brush your teeth. Keep a Bible in the bathroom for an easy reach. Highlight the words and thoughts on praise in your Bible. When you skim through a passage, read the highlighted words. Purpose in your heart to praise God through these readings, and allow them to sink in to your spirits. Most hymns are written from Scripture. Make a list of hymns you know and begin to lift those phrases that come directly from the Bible. Some phrases may not come verbatim from Scripture, but they do express thoughts of praise. Praise should flow from a Christian's heart very freely. You have to practice. Here are some expressions of thanksgiving:

Thank You	Grateful Heart	Salvation
Grace	Wholeness	Love
Mercy	Covenant	Loving
Kindness	Goodness	Blood
Saving Power	Righteousness	
Deliverance	Covering	

These words denote our gratefulness to Jesus for saving us by the shedding of His blood. That blood cleanses us and covers us. We are grateful to be able to wear Jesus' blood as a cloak of righteousness. He died so that we might be made whole. He has been merciful to us and we will forever praise Him because He is good. Included in your list should also be other names by which God is called. It is not an exhaustive list:

Jehovah	Shepherd	High Tower
Almighty	Friend	Master
Fortress		
Rock	Comforter	Great I Am
Savior	Provider	Deliverer
King of Kings	Counselor	Ancient of Days
Teacher	Jesus	Keeper
Lord of Lords	Lover of my Soul	Abba
Shield and Buckler	Prince of Peace	First and Last
Beginning and the End	Holy One	Lamb
Alpha and Omega	Father	Friend

Use these names when you are in praise and worship. The names in themselves evoke power. It's a privilege to be able to use them. Use them to denote His place in your heart during a particular storm or conflict in your life.

This next list is one of descriptors that describe the character of God:

Mighty	Faithful	Wonderful
Marvelous	Righteous	Powerful
Awesome	Holy	Good
Excellent	Just	Great
Worthy	Merciful	Omniscient
Gracious	Omnipotent	Omnipresent
Glorious	Royal	Majestic

Use these descriptors to brag and boast about your God. He loves when His children tell of His excellence and mercy. You know that He is worthy! Then **"Let the redeemed of the Lord say so..."** (Psalm 107:2). This language may be used during praise and worship.

The next is a list of verbs that express how we feel toward God:

Praise	Love	Bless	Worship
Honor	Exalt	Rejoice	Delight
Magnify	Yearn	Glorify	Long
Adore	Extol	Reverence	Bow

This group of words expresses how God makes us feel toward Him:

Grateful   Loved
Joyful   Cherished
Blessed
Thankful

This should be our attitude and main purpose in coming to worship Him. When we lift His name, He lifts us to greater heights. What an awesome privilege it is to fellowship with the greatest power in the universe. There is no one greater than God. This should be your joy, your passion, and your purpose for living. That's why He created you.

The more you practice this language everyday, the more it becomes a part of you. You might have to read them in the beginning, but they will attach themselves to your spirit. Eventually, you will be able to speak paragraphs about your God very fluently. It depends on your hunger. Anything you hunger for will become your passion. You must purpose in your heart to have a passion for God. Being filled with the Holy Spirit will help you to build that passion.

Chapter 5
What Does Worship Look Like?

Well, if praise generates excitement, then worship
generates passion and a longing to see God not for
what He has done, but for who He is. His greatness
is inconceivable. Worship is God's response to our
seeking after Him. We want God to find us. It is
during worship that this happens. When we think of
who He is in all His glory, and we look at who we
are, there should be longing to know Him and why
He even wants to have a relationship with us.

God is so big, and we are messed up. We need His
glory to cover us so we can begin to appreciate His
greatness and love for us. Worship produces a
response from God to the longing that is in our
hearts. When our spirit connects to the Holy Spirit,

you could say we just won the prize. God in His infinite wisdom draws us closer to Him, so that He can stroke us with His glory. This is the work of the Holy Spirit. Only He can draw us into the presence of God. As we begin to sing songs of worship, the Holy Spirit begins to move on our hearts. As we open up to Him, He pulls us into the presence of God. He does the work. Then the spirit-to-Spirit encounter begins. He tenderizes our hearts so that our faith in Him can soar, and we can say yes to anything He asks of us.

During worship, you would expect to see lifted hands, crying for joy, bowing in reverence, kneeling in adoration, and laying prostrate in humility. The music helps create an atmosphere, which will tone down the exuberant praise. Remember that praise is for the flesh and soul. Worship is done through the mind to open up the spirit to become more sensitive to the Holy Spirit. Through your will you must desire to experience God. We use our minds in conjunction with our words to create an atmosphere in our hearts. The Holy Spirit senses that we are ready and His power pulls us into the very presence of God.

It is important to consecrate yourself once again to God's will and plan for your life. It is also important to ask forgiveness and not harbor bitterness. You want the mind to be free from guilt and shame. Removing any obstacles that would hinder your entering in is a must. All pretense and fakery must be removed. You should be willing to stand naked before your God. He knows everything about you. He sees everything you have done.

The worship experience is a beautiful expression of love from our hearts to God. One might observe lifted hands as a song being sung. Again, if you don't understand what is being sung, then create your own expressions. Tell God what he means to you. Tell Him that you adore Him. Tell Him that you see Him clothed in royalty. The mind, the body, and the spirit are coming in agreement, and with the aid of the Holy Spirit, the worshipper will be drawn into God's presence if the condition of the heart is right.

During the worship experience, it is not appropriate to clap. You want to enter the chamber of your Lord, and so you come with adoration, longings, and a hunger. You begin to talk sweetly to your

Savior and love Him with words from a song or from your heart. His glory might compel you to bow, kneel, or even lay prostrate. When was the last time you knelt before God? I'm not speaking about pray, but to worship. These physical acts are merely an indication of what you are feeling in your heart. You can perform them right at your seat in the pew or at the altar. Linger there and continue to stroke your Lord with your words, as your heart is lifted up toward heaven. He will begin to flood your soul or mind with His glory. Worship is reverencing your God. You are now in position to "press in."

Worship generally produces an emotion that can be witnessed by others. You might cry, moan, cry out, or even speak in your prayer language (I address this in another chapter). It is climatic as your passion and love for God builds, and there is a quiet release and a desire to bask in His glory as you quietly wait for a word, a revelation, or simply His peace. God speaks to brokenness. I reiterate again here that clapping is not appropriate. At this point, you are more in awe of Him and His glory than shouting or clapping. Look at the woman with the alabaster box of oil sitting at Jesus' feet. This was not a time to dance, but a time to release all that was in her to Christ. In doing so, her heart was yielded to Him, which produced tears as she worshipped Him (Luke 7:37-38).

Some worship leaders will exhort you to clap, because they don't know what else to do. Others will ask you to "press in" or "keep going" with your worship language, but the people don't know how. This is something you cannot fake, and yelling through the microphone will not get you there. The worship experience is a process that takes more time for some to experience. It takes a hunger for God, experiences, trials, victories, and a repentant heart. Worship cannot be forced. When the timing is right, the only thing that can get you there is a heart that is broken, words to express what is in your heart, and a mind that is fixed on Jesus.

It would be appropriate here for the musicians to play softly and allow the Holy Spirit to do His work. The atmosphere should not be clouded by the singers taking the spotlight. At this time, there could be a gentle word of encouragement by the praise leader or pastor, but done very softly. The Holy Spirit has the spotlight now. With an atmosphere that is charged with the glory of God, the Holy

Spirit is now free to exercise the will of the Father. He can use His servants to minister deliverance or he can move on the hearts of the people Himself. Here the pastor can exhort the people to make their declaration of their desires or make their request for healing or deliverance. You are in the presence of the living God, and in position to speak to an open heaven. It might not be God's timing for your deliverance, but you are in a position to pull on God's grace as He sees your heart mixed with faith.

We see an example of pulling on God when Jesus' mother, Mary, made a request of Him before He had started His public ministry. She asked Him to change the water into wine at the wedding in Cana of Galilee. Mary was in the presence of God and her faith provoked Jesus to honor her request (John 2:1-9). Again, we see an example of someone making a demand on God through faith when the Canaanite woman came to Jesus for a miracle for her daughter, and Jesus told her that He was sent only to the House of Israel. He called her a dog and that she could not take the children's bread. The term dog here refers to anyone who was not Jewish. She told Him that even the dogs eat the crumbs that fall from the table. She was in the presence of God, and her faith made a demand on Jesus (Matthew 15:22-28). He honored her request and cures her daughter. We see that in God's presence anything can happen, even before it's seasoned to occur. When you have everyone on one accord, the Holy Spirit is free to do whatever He desires as He sees your heart open and yielded. At this point, the Word may or may not even be preached. This is called "Letting the Lord have His way." How many times have you witnessed this?

1 Kings 8:11 declares, **"And it came to pass, when the priests were come out of the holy place, that the cloud filled the house of the Lord, so that the priests could not stand to minister because of the cloud: for the glory of the cloud had filled the house of the Lord."** During the temple worship, the high priests were only allowed to minister directly to God. Those of us who have received Jesus as Lord are now able to minister directly to God (1 Peter 2:5, 9). How would you like God to sweep you off your feet? I have experienced this, as well as other saints, and it is glorious. It has happened on many occasions right in my home but rarely in fellowship with the saints. There's not enough time allotted for seeking God's presence because the set

program takes precedence. Getting God's glory in the house is paramount to the worship experience. The preacher needs God's glory to effectively minister to the people. It is God's anointing on the preached word that brings conviction to the believer or sinner. Deliverance can come any time during the worship experience, during praise and worship, prayer, or the sermon, but God's glory must be in the house. Praise brings you out of worship. You are so grateful that God's glory came in the house and touched you that you want to express gratitude for His presence.

I have briefly tried to give you a picture of what worship looks like, but there is no real formula. I've given a pattern that I use to get into the presence of God. You might require something else. Your language might be uniquely different, but if it glorifies God, then He receives it. Music has a different affect on people and therefore they can have different reactions or emotions. The songs you sing might not be my choice, but if it brings adoration to Him, then He receives it. You have to spend quality time in the presence of God to understand how the Holy Spirit works with you. Christians are connected to the same God, but each one of us has a unique and individual relationship that comes from having different experiences. Remember that if the music being played or sung is not your choice, then use your own worship language to create the picture you need to reverence your God.

I don't have a formula, but I do have a roadmap. I can get you to the destination you are seeking, which is the presence of God if you want to go. Each of you may view different scenes, but they are all beautiful. The more you travel the road, the faster you get there, but I would rather enjoy the view while I'm traveling.

Desiring to enter into God's presence is not a free gift. It will cost you time, patience, perseverance, sincerity, honesty, and holy living. Because this is a lifestyle, you must constantly allow the Holy Spirit to cleanse you. Many are not willing to pay the price. You have to desire it and ask for help to achieve it. If there is a longing to know God more intimately, worshipping is something you can do. It gets easier as you practice. You get to a level where just thinking on Him can create an explosion in your heart.

Chapter 6
The Language of Worship

Just as praise has a sound or language, worship too has a language. This does not mean that you cannot use either at your discretion. I have included some of the same words from the praise list. This list is an aid to get started if you do not have the tools. Remember, there is no formula. I would suggest that you get your highlighter again and take a trip through the Book of Psalms and highlight those words that lift up God's name and His character. Read over the highlighted words every day so that they can sink deep down into your spirit. Tape a list to your mirror and memorize them. This is not an exhaustive list, but these words can express your

feelings toward God. You do not have to be shy
with God. He is One to be trusted with these
intimate thoughts and displays of affection. Use
words from this list daily during your prayer time:

Love	Worship	Long For	Peace
Lovely	Embrace	Lavish	Joy
Adore	Bow	Excellent	Hallelujah
Adoration	Kneel	Majesty	The Great I Am
Holy	Pant after	Royalty	Lord
I Love You	Reverence	Hunger for	Presence
Thirst For	All in All	Everything	

When these words come together, they create a
tremendous release of power to your spirit. The key
word is worship through adoration. When
worshipping, you are in awe of the Mighty One.
When Jesus healed someone, they bowed or knelt
before Him in reverence to Him. They did not dance
about nor do a holy shout. The woman who poured
oil on the feet of Jesus and then began to wipe His
feet with her hair was worshipping Him.

Obviously, women find it easier to do this, but I
have seen a few men weep and worship their King.
Women can love a male figure in the natural and so

this love is easily transferred to Jesus. Most men, on the other hand, do not see themselves embracing Jesus or desiring His touch. Some feel that too much emotion displayed is not manly, but men are a part of the body of Christ. They are a part of the bride that Jesus is coming for. Men have to remember that this connection is spiritual.

Again there is no formula. You must spend time desiring Him, and the Holy Spirit will use what you have to open up your spirit so that you can enter into the presence of God.

Chapter 7
The Work of the Holy Spirit

The Holy Spirit is God's agent operating in the world today. Jehovah God, our Creator, is seated in heaven, and Jesus Christ, our Lord and Savior, is seated at the right hand of the Father forever · making intercession for us (Romans 8:34). In John 1:33-34, John the Baptist spoke of the Holy Spirit when he spoke to the Pharisees and said, **"And I knew Him not: but He that sent me to baptize with water, the same said unto me, Upon which you see the Spirit (like a dove) descending and remaining on Him, the same is he which baptizeth with The Holy Ghost, And I saw,, and bare record of that this is the Son of God."** I will interject here that John the Baptist was already filled with the Holy Spirit from his mother's womb according to Luke 1:15. I'll also note that Jesus, according to Luke 4:1, was full of the Holy Spirit.

Let me briefly trace the promise of the Holy Spirit that Jesus spoke of. Before the death of Christ, Jesus told His disciples that He was going to pray to the Father to give them another Comforter to abide with them forever (John 14:16). This Comforter was also called the Spirit of Truth (John 14:17). In verse 26 of that same chapter, Jesus said, **"But the Comforter, which is the Holy Ghost, whom the father will send in my name, He shall teach you all things, and bring all things to your remembrance, whatsoever I have said unto you."** Jesus speaks again in John 16:7. In Luke 24:49, Jesus told His disciples to **"...but tarry ye in Jerusalem until ye be endued with power from on high."** In Acts 1: 8, Christ is quoted by saying, **"But ye shall receive power after the Holy Ghost is come upon you, and ye shall be witnesses unto me both in Jerusalem, and in all Judea, and in Samaria, and unto the uttermost part of the world."**

What is the Holy Spirit called?

Comforter: John 14:16; John 16:7; John 14:26

Spirit of Truth: John 14:17; John 15:26; John 16:13

Holy Ghost: John 14:26; John 15:26

What does the Holy Spirit do?

Testify of Christ: John 15:26

Reprove the world of sin (convict): John 16:8

Teach: John 15:26; Luke 12:12

Lead and guide: John 16:13

Show you things to come: John 16:13

Abide with you: John 14:16

Glorify Jesus: John 16:14

Look at all the things the Holy Spirit does. Wouldn't you want this power residing in you? When I discovered these truths, I asked for the gift. I was saved and loved Jesus, but I had no power. The Holy Spirit was sent by Jesus to comfort, to teach, to show, and to glorify God. The Holy Spirit is the representative of Christ. He did and does everything Jesus did when Jesus walked the Earth. Jesus completed His work on the cross, but He sent supernatural help in the form of the Holy Spirit. It is the working or power of the Holy Spirit that draws us into the presence of God. We do not worship the Holy Spirit. We submit to Him. The Holy Spirit always points us to Jesus. Our body is His temple, His place of residence. Jesus will come into your heart to save you. The Holy Spirit comes to make His abode or dwelling place in your body. 2 Corinthians 6:16 tells us that we become the temple of the Holy Ghost.

We see the initial entrance of the Holy Spirit in the earth on the day of Pentecost in the second chapter of Acts, verses 2-4. This promise descended from heaven like a mighty rushing wind. Peter preached a fiery sermon, and the people asked what they must do to be saved. He said in Acts 2:38-39 to **"Repent and be baptized every one of you in the name of Jesus Christ for the remission of sins, and ye shall receive the gift of the Holy Ghost. For the promise is unto you and to your children, and to all that are afar off, even as many as the Lord our God shall call."** The Holy Spirit is a gift, but you have to desire the gift. The gift is not thrust upon you. In Luke 11:13 Jesus said, **"If ye being evil, know how to give good gifts unto your children, how much more shall your heavenly Father give the Holy Spirit to them that ask Him."** In 2 Corinthians 1:20 it states, **"The promises of God in Him are yea and in Him amen."** God does not lie, so if He said that as a child of God we can to ask for the Holy Spirit, why not do so?

It is the Holy Spirit who is the agent in the earth today. He does the saving, the transforming, the healing, and the perfecting. He also guides us into the very presence of God. Remember, worship is spirit-to-Spirit. We cannot worship God with our flesh. Our hearts must be right with God first before we can enter into His presence. Worship is done through the Holy Spirit. Jesus told us that the time would come when the true worshippers would worship Him in Spirit and in truth: for the Father seeketh such to worship Him (John 4:23). **"God is a Spirit: and they that worship Him must worship Him in spirit and in truth"** (John 4: 24).

Many will say that when you come to Jesus that you are filled with the Holy Spirit then. Let's see what God's Word says. Yes, Jesus does come to dwell within you and begins to change your heart when you make Him Lord. In the Book of Acts, we see the beginnings of the Church with the disciples and new converts. It becomes quite clear that infilling or baptism of the Holy Spirit was a different action from becoming born again. The disciples were already believers in Christ Jesus, but Jesus told them not to do anything until they received power from on high (Luke 24:49) and (Acts 1:8). There were other believers in Acts who had never even heard about the Holy Ghost. They had received Jesus, but not the Holy Ghost (Acts 19:2-6).

> In Acts 19:2-6, Paul is speaking to certain disciples: **"He said unto them, have you received the Holy Ghost since ye believed? And they said we have not so much as heard whether there be any Holy Ghost. And he said unto them, Unto what then were ye baptized? And they said, Unto John's baptism. Then said Paul, John verily baptized with the baptism of**

repentance, saying to the people, that they should believe on Him, which should come after Him that is on Jesus Christ. When they heard this, they were baptized in the name of the Lord Jesus. And then Paul laid his hands upon them, the Holy Ghost came upon them, and they spake with tongues and prophesied."

It is clear in the Book of Acts that these believers of Christ were not filled or baptized with the Holy Spirit. They knew Christ but were not acquainted with the Holy Ghost. They were saved, but they did not have the power given through the Holy Spirit. What about you? The saving grace of Jesus dwells in you, but do you have the power of the Holy Spirit abiding in you to teach, to convict, to witness, and to glorify (worship) Jesus?

The resounding theme in the Book of Acts is the infilling or the baptism of the Holy Spirit with the evidence of speaking in tongues. This is the proof that you are filled with the Holy Spirit. Let's reiterate. The Holy Spirit is not to be feared or shunned but to be embraced. Even Jesus was filled with the Holy Ghost when led into the desert to be tempted of the Satan (Luke 4:1). John the Baptist was filled with Holy Spirit in his mother's womb (Luke 1:15). The disciples in the upper room were filled with Holy Ghost (Acts 2:4).Why? In each scenario they needed the power to complete the task God wanted them to do.

Jesus commissioned the disciples to **"Go ye therefore, and teach all nations, baptizing them in the name of the Father, and of the Son, and of the Holy Ghost. Teaching them to observe all things whatsoever I have commanded you: and, lo, I am with you always, even unto the end of the world"** (Matthew 2:19, 20). Jesus spoke in Mark 16:17, **"And these signs shall follow them that believe: In my name they shall cast out devils; they shall speak with new tongues."** Again, in Luke 24:49, Jesus said, **"And, behold, I send the promise of my Father upon you: but tarry ye in the city of Jerusalem, until ye be endued with power from on high"**.

Are you a disciple of Jesus Christ? Then you also need His power to do what God has called you to do. Read the following scriptures to get a sense of what happened after the coming of the Holy Spirit fell on one hundred and twenty people who were waiting for Him to come as Jesus had commanded.

- Acts 10:44—Holy Ghost fell on them which heard
- Acts 9:17—Paul was filled with the Holy Spirit
- Acts 6:5—Stephen full of faith and the Holy Ghost
- Acts 8:15-17—People in Samaria received the Holy Ghost
- Acts 11:22—Barnabas was full of the Holy Ghost
- Acts 13:52—Disciples were full of the Holy Ghost
- Acts 15:8—Gentiles were given the Holy Ghost

There are ministries that will pray and lay hands on you to receive the gift of the Holy Spirit from God.

Most deliverance ministries can assist you with this. No one laid their hands on me, however. I just asked God, and He saw my heart and desperation and gave me the gift of the Holy Spirit over twenty years ago while I was driving in my car after seeking Him for three weeks. The Holy Spirit delivered me from fear of worshipping God in public, because I was not taught to do so. I never heard a sermon or teaching on praise and worship at that time. I was taught by the power of the Holy Spirit. I have never been the same. I have heard stories of others receiving the baptism while taking a shower or in their kitchen cooking. God Himself selects the time when He sees the readiness of the heart, a life committed to Him, and that His child is ready.

Are you a disciple of the Lord Jesus Christ? Then you too need to be filled with the Holy Spirit. This promise or gift is for you and your children (Acts 2:38-39). The Holy Spirit is here now to minister to you. You must empty out of yourself, so that you can make room for Him. Empty yourself of your desires and fears, and submit to whatever He desires. This dying of the self must become an act of your free will. God will not force you. You must prefer Him and His purposes to anything or anyone else. You can be filled right now. This baptism is a gift. God knows that you cannot complete this journey without help, but that you need supernatural empowerment, given through the Holy Spirit, to defeat the enemy and bring glory to God.

Remember that **"For in Him we live, move, and have our being"** (Acts 17:28).

Chapter 8
Pressing In to Enter In

During the worship experience, some find it difficult to enter into God's presence. They are on the brink of entering, but they never arrive. There are sometimes hindrances that prevent the worshipper from the one-on-one encounter with God. These are some possible hindrances that should be dealt with:

- ➢ Unconfessed sin
- ➢ Unforgiveness
- ➢ Bitterness
- ➢ Witchcraft
- ➢ Religious Spirit
- ➢ Rebellion

- ➤ Disobedience
- ➤ Anger

A vessel is an instrument used to carry or hold something. God uses our bodies as vessels to carry His anointing to bring about truth, deliverance, love, salvation, and power. If we are full of ourselves, there leaves no room for Him to fill us. We must be willing to get rid of the junk we carry so that He can use us for His glory.

You must empty out of the self by repenting and denouncing any demonic connections by crying out to God for help or seeking a deliverance ministry to help rid your mind and heart from the demonic snares. God is holy and He will not contaminate Himself by communing with an unclean vessel. The condition of the heart must be dealt with first before He will allow you to enter into His presence.

After you have allowed God to reveal anything you are harboring in your heart, and you have asked for His forgiveness; God will lift the weight or burden you carry and give you peace about the situation. This process may not be immediate, so continue to

---

seek God for an answer. Remember, God is looking at your heart. He knows when you are sincere and ready. You will also know. Then you be can free to press or enter into His presence.

After you have praised God and thanked Him from the depths of your heart as your mind is fixed on Him, you can begin to worship through a song and by telling Him much you love Him. At some point you will feel broken and teary eyed. It is at that moment that you need to "press in." You might say, "You are so wonderful to me Jesus." Well, what else can you think to say? Then you could say, "I need you more than ever." Well, what else can you say? "Then you could say, "I need you to hold me close." Well, what else can you say? Then you could say, "You're my everything." I hope you understand what is happening here. You are building a platform for the Holy Spirit to work on your heart, and when it gets to the right plateau, you will begin to melt or break down and weep. I experience this over and over again. Then the Holy Spirit pulls you into God's presence. You lose sense of the natural, and God's glory sweeps over you, envelopes you, and saturates you. This is bliss as you fellowship spirit-to-Spirit. The loves that binds you together with Jesus is matchless.

Pressing in to enter in is simply laying on a thought and continuing to build upon that thought. It's almost like speaking a paragraph concerning how you feel about Jesus. Some people have a limited vocabulary when it comes to actually worshipping God. They can say, "God is good," but they cannot build upon that statement. When you press in, you must build a platform with your words and thoughts to paint a picture for the Holy Spirit to use to melt your heart. These words and thoughts are what I call "triggers." Your love and adoration for Jesus is just one "trigger" that can begin the "press." My press is not your press. You must learn to build your own. It's more effective when the press comes from your own heart and soul. This is why I included a chapter on the language of worship, which will assist you in communing with God.

Another "trigger" could be remembering "from whence you came" and acknowledging that Jesus covered those sins with His blood. So the press might go like this:

"Lord, I love you so much. I was in the pit about ready to sink. You reached down and picked me up. I don't deserve your love, but I'm sure glad you remembered me. I owe you my life. I will praise your name forever and ever. You are the best thing that has ever happened to me. What can I do for you? Whatever you want me to do, I'm willing to do. You are my everything."

This definitely is a "trigger" for me, because I'm crying even now as I write. When you know what He has done for you personally, it becomes easy to love on Him and worship Him. A "trigger" is a picture or thought you can use to build upon that opens up your heart to receive the Holy Spirit.

This last 'trigger" is another example of what I use to help me enter into the presence of God. You must discover yours. Remember, there is no formula. It takes a desire and time alone with God to allow the Holy Spirit to teach you what He already knows about you. Remember, He is the teacher.

"Jesus, you are my one and only love. Thank you for loving me. You willingly gave your life that I would be set free. My sins nailed you to the cross too. I'm sorry that they beat you and cursed you, but I'm glad that you didn't come down from the cross. You were innocent, but willing to take my place. Thank you for changing me and making me whole. My will is to do your will. Receive my love. I lavish it all on you."

The "triggers" I use are always different. It is never a script. When you begin to bare your soul and actually remember what God delivered you from, the melting process begins. The words always come from my heart. The Holy Spirit gives me new and fresh ideas everyday that I have never expressed before. This comes from time sitting in His presence and singing to Jesus. The Holy Spirit gives me new songs. I dance with Jesus. It's usually a waltz. Start wherever you need to start. If you need a script to begin, then do so. You are practicing the presence of God. This practice for individuals could be at home where you would have more time. I could see this practice being done at a midweek service before Bible study. Yes, I could see it even at a morning worship service. As I minister, I teach on worship through demonstration and participation. In this way, the people can immediately practice the things that they have heard.

Chapter 9
Warring Against the Mind

Those of you reading this book might say, "I just cannot press my way through to God." There may be some fleshy barriers that need to be addressed. The flesh is powerful, but one's thoughts are even more powerful. Here I am asking you to love on Jesus, and many would find it difficult to use words of affection toward their spouse. Many Christians are not in touch with their emotions and would rather hide them or become numb to them. Just remember it was God who created these emotions, and He wants you to use them to gain access to Him. How badly do you want Him? The Holy Spirit cannot complete His work if you do not submit to

His provisions for drawing you closer to Him. **"The sacrifices of God are a broken spirit: a broken and contrite heart, O God, Thou wilt not despise"** (Psalm 51:17).

Some might interpret tears or crying for weakness and associate it with sadness, death, pain, suffering, and a lack of control. You hear a baby cry and assume it is hungry or in need of a diaper change. Your crying child comes running into the house with a bloody knee, and you know he is in pain. Your loved one dies and you shed tears from the loss. You might even entertain the notion that tears are an indication that one is mentally unfit and suggests that one is out of control. Children cry after a scolding, and the parent quickly reprimands them to stop. Men are certainly admonished to keep a stiff upper lip. You see a movie and it saddens you. One might stifle the tears to appear to be unmoved. We need to come to grips with our traditional thoughts on crying. It has been given a bad reputation. Even though crying can be a result of the above, it has far greater significance. What does crying really do?

Crying in the natural is a release mechanism, whether it is anger, joy, or pain. Tension or energy builds up in the body as muscles stiffen and tighten. Crying is a natural way to release that tension and allow the body to regain its normalcy. Usually one feels better after a good cry.

The Holy Spirit uses these tears when you give your heart to Christ. As the Holy Spirit draws a sinner, He uses tears to massage the stony heart. He massages that heart until it becomes soft, pliable, and yielding. The supernatural work turns the stony heart into a heart that is fleshy and can therefore submit to God.

Let's look at an example of worship in the New Testament with the woman who came with the alabaster oil and anointed the feet of Jesus. First, she washed His feet with her tears, wiped them with her hair, and kissed His feet (Luke 7:38). Even though she was a sinner, being in the presence of Jesus forever transformed her. Her heart was repentant and her mind was fixed on Jesus. She was condemned by the Pharisees and blessed by our

Lord. Jesus accepted this act of worship because her heart was right.

This was a true act of worship. She came broken and knelt at the feet of Jesus. It does not indicate that she spoke, but she did something very special. She brought a costly gift. The best gift we can bring is to offer up the sacrifice of praise from our lips (Hebrews 13:5). Praise from our lips is like a sweet smelling fragrance to God. Open up your mouth and tell Him that you love Him. She knelt before the Lord even at the criticism of others. Rarely do you see one kneel at a service. She wept as she worshipped and washed the feet of Christ with her hair. She was releasing her total being to Christ. When we worship, there should be a total release of ourselves to Him by coming with a pure and broken heart. This was an intense moment for this woman, who was out of place with man but in touch with the Master. Being in the presence of God is life changing. This is why worship is so important.

While you are worshipping God, the condition of your heart is very important. It needs to be broken, so it is soft, pliable, and wanting. A heart that is hardened cannot enter into God's presence. As the tears are released, the Holy Spirit uses them to soften the heart and make it ready to receive Jesus. Your words of adorations assist the Holy Spirit in doing His job. It's in the "press" that the tears, the words, and softened heart all come together and the Holy Spirit knows when to pull you in. In His presence there is no pain, no fear, and no lack.

His presence overshadows everything. You lose sight of self as His glory permeates your being. Your faith is increased, because there is no struggle. You can say yes to your Master. This is truly a glorious experience. No two encounters are alike. Now you can understand why Satan uses the traditions of men to prevent you from wanting to enter God's presence. It doesn't look dignified. Some Christians always want to be in complete control. You must relinquish that control to the Holy Spirit. Satan has deceived many in thinking that it does not take all of this to worship God. Some would say that it takes too much time. Short teachings, along with demonstrations from leadership, will assist those who are hungry for God. But I dare you to try it for yourself. How do I know these things? The Holy Spirit is the teacher. **"…He will guide you into all truth"** (John 16:13).

As you can see, the shedding of tears can be a good thing. Tears are often observed at joyous occasions also. Marriage is a time when many would shed tears of joy. The birth of a child can produce floods of joy. A job promotion might also produce joy and excitement, and the tears might flow freely. These examples of joy demonstrated through tears are accepted in our society. However, one might desire not to linger for any length of time. We still have a tendency to stifle or cut the emotion short.

Likewise, sitting in the presence of God produces a flood of emotion, but you want to stay there. Let me say that again: You want to stay there. Do not stifle the emotions that are building up. There is no hurry to leave as you allow God the opportunity to deliver, speak, heal, or give His peace. This is a good thing. His glory rubs off on you as you commune with Him. Your faith is increased, and you come into agreement with His plans for you. All of this can happen in His presence whether you are in a service or worshipping alone. But this will require practicing His presence. How hungry are you?

God has given us a mind to think on Him. He has given us a memory to go back and recall His goodness toward us. God has given us a tongue to praise Him. God has given us emotions and tears to worship, which draws us closer to Him. We must learn to use all of the gifts and abilities God has given to us. We use them in our everyday lives to enjoy God's abundant creation and discover new dimensions of life. How much more should we use our emotions to gain access to Him through worship?

Chapter 10
The Musicians and Praise Team or Choir

Singers and musicians that are anointed and called of God have an awesome responsibility of acting as a conduit or carrier of the anointing of God. Music is an integral part of any service. Remember, these are the gifts we use to usher us into the presence of God, so their positions should not be taken lightly. We need the presence of God in the house so that people can be saved, healed, and delivered. God's presence is paramount. In the Garden of Eden, Adam did not have a preacher, a choir, or musician, but he did have access to the presence of God.

As you read this book, you will realize that some issues do not apply to you. Attend to the issues that are problematic in your congregation. I understand that new ministries will often accept anyone with talent who can sing or play to be apart of a ministry. However, pastors should not be deceived into thinking that anyone can perform these duties and indulge in any kind of lifestyle. You often see musicians coming in late with no passion for what they are doing. They simply go through the rudiments of their craft without even acknowledging God. Pastors should always be leading those gifted in the music ministry to Christ and then to the infilling of the Holy Spirit.

My belief is that pastors sometimes feel they will lose these musicians if they press them too hard about living a sanctified life. It is also a well-known fact that trained musicians and ministers of music are generally paid for their services. In many cases, the talent or position is coveted more than the person's character. In other words, any behavior is tolerated because the person is very talented. We need gifted people in the music ministry who are sold out to Jesus Christ and can flow in the spirit with the Holy Ghost, and not just hirelings.

When you have a music team where every member has been filled with the Holy Spirit, then supernatural things can occur. The Holy Spirit can bring forth the right selection, instrumentally, for the congregation so that He can move on their hearts. He can also create a new song that will bring forth a more powerful anointing to break yokes. All of this can be done because He has a team flowing and moving in Him. I experienced this once. The minister of music and I created a song through the leading of the Holy Spirit, and everyone in the house was blessed as they stood to their feet acknowledging the presence of God. What the Holy Spirit had produced, we could not reproduce.

Members of the music ministry should be meeting together not to just practice, but to worship and pray. They are in an awesome position to help impact the lives of those in the congregation. The pastor should speak with each member of the music ministry to find out where they currently are in their faith and what their goals are. He should explain what his vision is for the ministry and where they fit in. When the leadership and music ministry are on one accord, then the ministry can usher in the presence of God so that He can truly be exalted. None of us are perfect, but those who love the Lord should be pressing for the mark of the high calling in Christ Jesus (Philippians 3:14) and allow the Holy Spirit to conform us to the image of Christ (Romans 3:29). They too should desire to grow into mature Christians through the transforming power of the Holy Spirit.

The praise team should ultimately be born again and filled with the Holy Ghost. Pastors initially might accept willing singers, but there should be an expectation of growth through Bible study and a commitment to the vision of the ministry.

Attire is very important, especially for the women. There should not be distractions because of the length of skirts, the tightness of a dress, or exposure of the chest. How can you lead a congregation in the spirit when the focus is on the flesh? If proper attire is not possible, then leadership should step in and provide it. Members of the praise team should ultimately exhibit modesty in their behavior, as well as their dress. God is seeking vessels of honor through which He can fill, flow through, and use for His glory.

Some of the issues described are not a matter of right or wrong, but what pleases God. Our worship should reflect what He desires because ultimately, the benefits of doing it God's way outweigh our programs or desires.

The Cycle of Worship

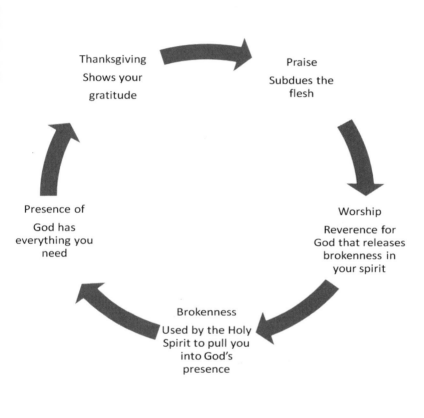

Thanksgiving
Shows your
gratitude

Praise
Subdues the
flesh

Worship
Reverence for
God that releases
brokenness in
your spirit

Brokenness
Used by the Holy
Spirit to pull you
into God's
presence

Presence of
God has
everything you
need

Figure 2.

Chapter 11
One-on-One Practice Time

This is a pattern, not a formula. You can use this to get started on your quest of seeking God's presence.

❖ Ask Jesus to fill you with the Holy Spirit. The Holy Spirit is your helper. Your infilling could take place during the worship experience. The Holy Spirit is a gift given to those who believe in Jesus. Attend a fellowship that ministers deliverance and believes in the laying on of hands to impart the gift. Be relentless until you are blessed.

❖ Select a time, either early or later, where you will have a minimum of distractions.

❖ Center yourself with a fixed mind on Christ through a short prayer of consecration and ask God to forgive and cleanse you from all unrighteousness.

❖ Thank Jesus for saving you and begin to praise Him for the things He has already done for you. Name the blessings He has given you. Clear the atmosphere with words of thanksgiving.

❖ Sing a few songs of praise to your God with or without a musical recording.

❖ Walk around and clap your hands with joy and enthusiasm, and shout for the victory that is already won.

❖ Use your praise language and brag and boast about your God keeping your mind on Him and avoiding distractions.

❖ Continue to praise and thank Him. Use your prayer language.

❖ Now begin to worship Him for whom He is. Use your worship language to express your feeling about His greatness.

❖ Sing a love or tender song to Him and ask for His glory to sweep over you.

❖ Begin to build your platform of worship by talking and loving on Him. Use any triggers you have to assist you. Remember, this talk must become a platform whereby you can "press in."

❖ The moment you begin to swell up or become teary eyed continue with the press.

❖ The Holy Spirit needs this to melt the heart. As the tears begin to flow, He will use their release to pull you into the presence of God.

❖ You will know when you are there, because you will be crying and thanking Jesus uncontrollably. The Holy Spirit will speak through you, and you will not be lost for words.

❖ At some point you will be compelled to bow, kneel, or lie prostrate before Him as He sweeps over you. This is pure bliss, and you want to linger a while. You can even sing or speak in your prayer language. What the Holy Spirit is doing is sweeping you off your feet. How glorious!

❖ You might be compelled to declare that He is yours and you are His. You may even inquire if there is anything you can do for Him, because He has done everything for you. Again, the Holy Spirit will move on you and speaking will be made easy.

❖ You are in a position to speak directly to God. There will be a peace that surpasses all understanding. Joy bells will ring. All you know is that you want to please Him. The things that were difficult in the natural are made easy in the spirit.

❖ Anything can take place while you are in His presence, so just be sensitive to Jesus.

❖ You can begin to praise Jesus as you come out of worship and thanking

Him for the privilege of allowing
you to be in His presence.

❖ You can go into prayer or sing a
song from your spirit. I usually have
communion and then intercessory
prayer.

If by chance you are unable to enter in, try again the
next day. Make it your heart's desire to continue
until you do enter in. It is in the trials that you will
begin to learn what it takes for you to achieve your
goal. The Holy Spirit will teach you. Anyone who
chases after God will find Him.

The worship experience can last as long as you can
endure the blissful moments. This time is emotional
and consuming. My worship and prayer time might
be an hour. This is personal, and any time you
spend will not be wasted time. It's your turn. This
experience is available to all who want it. If there is
something stirring in you now, the Holy Spirit is
here right now to assist you. Do you need to confess
any sin? Do you need to repent of any sin? Do you
need to be filled with the Holy Spirit? Now would

be a good time to open up your heart and cry out for help. The Holy Spirit is always ready to work. If you have been running after God, today could be your life-changing moment to allow the Holy Spirit to snatch you up into the heavenlies. I promise you that you will not be let down.

Chapter 12
Corporate Worship

The devotional or praise and worship leader should always begin with a prayer of consecration for the people. Always remind the people why they are here. We want God's glory in the house, and we need everyone present to assist us. God's presence can mean salvation, deliverance, and healing for anyone who is ready for God to move into their lives. Only God knows if this is the hour you have been praying for, so we want to allow God to be God all by Himself. If you have latecomers who feel they can miss the time set aside to worship God collectively, you might have to remind them at some point of this opportunity to collectively usher in the presence of God. The pastor should participate in some part of the praise and worship experience. The congregation should be able to observe their pastors opening themselves up to God. They should look undignified too.

- ❖ Introduce each song with exhortations about Jesus and set the tone for each song sung.

- ❖ Do not allow the musicians to overpower the singing, for the people will not be able to hear themselves speak.

- ❖ After each song is sung, encourage the congregation to speak personally to God. Ultimately, this is what you want. The songs of praise are just an instrument to help instruct the people to what they should be doing and that is speaking to God.

- ❖ Yes, you can ask them to clap their hands, but do not allow the clapping to go on for an extended period of time. Always give time to allow them to speak to God personally.

❖ Use yourself as an example, and the people will follow. It is not necessary to yell or feel that you must coerce the people.

❖ The musicians should be playing in the background but not overpowering.

❖ During this time of celebration, invite the saints to dance and be jubilant in their praise. Some congregations provide banners and extra instruments for the saints to use at this grand time.

❖ There is usually a shift in the spirit realm, and the leader will sense that it is now time to begin to worship God.

❖ Introduce each worship song and lift up exhortations to your God for who He is.

❖ After each song, give time for the congregants to speak to God personally. Lead by example as you speak to God, and they will catch on and do the same.

- ❖ As you are being led by the Holy Spirit, let the musicians play alone as you continue to talk to God, and you will know when to begin the press. You cannot wait for everyone to enter in, because everyone is not on the same level.

- ❖ The press requires you to continue to build that platform using your worship language for those who might not yet know how.

- ❖ You can bow or kneel before the people to show them what they should be doing. The musicians should be playing softly and allowing the Holy Spirit to move on their playing.

- ❖ The psalmist could minister to God at this time. A psalmist is not a soloist. The psalmist does not minister or sing to the congregation. A psalmist sings to God. A psalmist does not perform. A psalmist is a yielded vessel used by God to carry the anointing. As the psalmist ministers to God, the congregation receives the overflow of the anointing.

❖ At this point there should be weeping and moaning, and the pastor or minister should then thank the Holy Spirit for His presence and to have His way. Tell God that you need Him here today. Expect a move of God. The pastor could then exhort the people to ask of God what they desire. Some ministers lay hands on the people as the Holy Spirit directs.

❖ I will mention here that at some fellowships, some pastors will minister directly to the people after the preached word. The praise is usually not as high as it is at the beginning of the service. The saints are tired and don't usually put out the energy needed to saturate the atmosphere with praise. Sometimes the choir is used at this point. Be directed by the Holy Spirit as to where you want to place the ministry of the Holy Spirit. Some make room at the beginning of the service, and others place the ministry of the Holy Spirit after the preached word. I am of the opinion that the ministry of the Holy Spirit is most effective when the praise and worship service is at its peak.

❖ Give God this time to move upon the people. Of course God has the liberty throughout the service to move as He so desires. Isn't it wonderful to know that you can actually give time for God to do what He does best?

❖ God comes to the saints (that is a spirit-to-Spirit connection), who are expecting Him. God can move in a sovereign way to bring glory to His name or for a specific purpose and the congregation gets blessed in spite of those who refuse to participate. However, He needs a band of saints who are sold out to Him that can usher in His presence whereby others can get delivered even though they themselves are unable to enter in. They can still receive the benefits of God's manifested glory.

❖ No two worship experiences are alike. Do not try to mimic what you sang or said before. Be sensitive to the Holy Spirit. He may give specific instructions. Stay in the Spirit, and do not let the time factor usurp His leadings.

❖ God allows those who expect to see Him to enter in. God's presence can manifest in a service, but not all Christians will be able to participate. They know God's there, but their spirits are not open to receive.

❖ The worship experience should end with praise unto God for His visitation with an expectation that you are eagerly awaiting His presence again.

Chapter 13
In Conclusion

I pray after digesting some of the concepts in this
book that your spirit has been enlightened. You
might need to revisit some chapters. You may need
to pray over others. Remember that this book is for
those who are seeking a deeper relationship with
God. The hunger is there, the heart is pliable, and
the spirit is ready—you just need to connect the
dots to get the broader picture of why we should
praise our God and what praise looks like.

I have tried to paint a picture for you. Praise does
not look pretty to the observer, but to the

participant, it is life altering. Your praise will bless God, and others might catch a few droplets of the overflow.

The praise and worship experience is more than uplifted hands or kneeling. To do them with bitterness in your heart, unforgiveness toward others, and unconfessed sin to God is just going through the motions. You will never achieve the height of euphoria that comes as a result of entering the presence of the living God. Many dance, cry, and shout during service, then return home to a life of sin with a live- in mate, viewing pornography on the computer or drug addictions. Yes, they love Jesus, but they are still in the flesh. In order to enter into the presence of God, the flesh must die, so that the spirit can connect to the Holy Spirit. You cannot continue a life of sin and waltz into God's presence. His presence will convict you and then deliver you. You cannot have it both ways. God wants His glory to consume you in order to change your life so that you can help advance His Kingdom. God's glory on your life will draw others to Him. You will not look dignified in His presence, because you must want to be consumed. When you are consumed, you relinquish all rights of the body, soul, and spirit.

We must have a fear or respect for Jehovah to the point where we recognize what His grace really means. This unmerited favor should catapult us to a position where we do not want to offend the One who took our place on Calvary. Grace should not give us license to continue in sin, but a desire to overcome sin. We should hate sin the way God hates sin. That is why sin must be confessed. If you are still having problems entering into the presence of God, there is a reason. God wants to commune with you more than you will ever know. He had me to write this book to break down some barriers and misunderstandings and make things clearer. I pray that these teachings have clarified some issues. The Holy Spirit is working on your heart right now. God wants you to be honest and real with Him. The Word declares, **"And ye shall know the truth and the truth shall make you free"** (John 8:32). Truth comes from within your spirit. The Holy Spirit will shine a light on that truth and you will know it. Get into God's presence, and let the truth ring loud and clear. Be blessed of the Lord as you make it your quest and soul desire to seek Him with all you heart, soul, and, mind. His presence is for all who desire it, for that was His intention from the beginning. Remember that His presence is full of joy, and at His right hand there are pleasures forever more (Psalm 16:11).

 Bibliography

Gibbs, Alfred. *Worship: The Christians Highest Occupation*. Kansas City: Walterick Publishers, 1950; 2012.

Luck, Coleman, G. *The Bible Book by Book.* Chicago: Moody Press, 1955.

Strong, James. *Strong's Exhaustive Concordance of the Bible.* World Bible Publishers, 1980; 1986.

Prayer of Salvation

If you are a reader and have not asked Jesus the come into
your heart and save you, you can do so now. You might be
someone who is unsure of your salvation. If you have decided
to make Jesus your choice, then pray this prayer:

**Father God, I am a sinner and need to be
saved. I repent of all my sins. I believe
that you sent your Son to die for me so
that my sins would be forgiven.
I ask you now Jesus to come into my
heart and save me. I ask you to fill me
with the Holy Spirit so that I can live holy
for you. Thank you for saving me. I pray
for you to direct my path and I will follow
in it. In Jesus I pray. Amen.**

Praise God! Praise God! You have just made a life-altering
decision. I pray that you will find a Bible teaching fellowship
where the presence of God is evident, and you can grow using
the gifts that God has planted in you.

Contact Information

Dr. Jennifer Gaither looks forward to ministering at your workshops or seminars. This is a hands-on ministry. I teach, demonstrate, and then the participants participate. Also, orders for books may be placed using the information below.

In His Presence Ministry

6107 Hopeton Avenue

Baltimore, MD 21215

410-358-3360

Fax: 410-358-3331

Email: jenrodus@yahoo.com